MAN'S INHUMANITIES

RACISM AND INTOLERANCE

By Charles E. Pederson

ERICKSON PRESS

Yankton, South Dakota

For more information, contact:
Erickson Press
329 Broadway
PO Box 33
Yankton, SD 57078

Or you can visit our Web site at **www.ericksonpress.com**

Content Consultant:
Professor Mark Bernstein
Joyce and Edward E. Brewer Chair in Applied Ethics
Philosophy Department, Purdue University

Editor: Amy Van Zee
Copy Editor: Paula Lewis
Design and Production: Becky Daum

Library of Congress Cataloging-in-Publication Data
Pederson, Charles E.
  Racism and intolerance / by Charles E. Pederson.
    p. cm. — (Man's inhumanities)
  Includes bibliographical references (p.   ) and index.
  ISBN 978-1-60217-976-9 (alk. paper)
1. Racism—Juvenile literature. 2. Racism—United States—Juvenile
literature. 3. Toleration—Juvenile literature. I. Title. II. Series.

HT1521.P39 2009
305.8—dc22

2008034829

CONTENTS

Introduction: Stories of Hatred 4

Chapter 1: What Is Racism? 7

Chapter 2: Prejudice and Stereotypes 16

Chapter 3: U.S. Racism and
African Americans 23

Chapter 4: U.S. Racism and Intolerance
Toward Other Groups 34

Chapter 5: Dealing with Racism
and Intolerance 45

Glossary 56

More Information 58

Notes 59

Index 62

About the Author 64

STORIES OF HATRED

Just before World War II, a group called the Nazis ruled Germany. They passed laws against Jewish people. Jews could not teach in universities, perform onstage, or practice law. They were also denied the right to vote. With all the freedoms enjoyed today in the United States, such discrimination seems outrageous.

But what about this story of hatred? In 1955, Emmett Till was a 14-year-old African American from Chicago. He went to visit his cousins and great-uncle in Mississippi. Emmett and his cousins went to a store. He spoke to the white woman who ran the shop. Several days later, on August 28, 1955, two white men kidnapped Emmett. Three days later he was found dead in a nearby river. He had been severely beaten and shot in the head. Two white men were arrested. A local jury of white men said the men did not

commit the crime. The men were set free. Later, the men admitted to being the killers. Some people said that Emmett had whistled at the white woman. The men killed Emmett because of this.

At the beginning of World War II, Jews were forced to wear patches on their clothes that designated them as Jews.

These events have one thing in common. They show behaviors of one group toward another based on physical differences. The behaviors were based on racist beliefs.

For centuries, people have been brutally hurt and unfairly treated because of their race. The issue of racism is not easy to deal with. It is not always

Emmett Till was brutally murdered for whistling at a white woman.

easy to define. Racism is directly related to intolerance. Intolerance means treating others with hate or with unwillingness to grant them rights. Racism and intolerance are complex issues.

Chapter 1

WHAT IS RACISM?

*T*he news media—television, radio, the Internet, and newspapers—have many stories about people hating and mistreating others. The treatment ranges from name-calling to violence. Some people even kill others. Racism and intolerance are specific kinds of mistreatment. The Merriam-Webster dictionary defines racism as: "a belief that race is the primary determinant of human traits . . . and that racial differences produce an inherent superiority of a particular race."[1]

Until the 1950s and 1960s, white control over blacks and other minority groups was widely accepted in the United States. All branches and levels of government supported it. Minorities were denied their civil rights. This took away their chance to play a part in politics. It kept them from earning more money or being part of some communities. Eugene Burnett,

The Ku Klux Klan is an extremely controversial society that still holds meetings today.

an African-American man, described his experience. After World War II, he wanted to buy a house in Levittown, New York. This was a new, beautiful suburb. He approached the salesman and inquired about purchasing one of the homes. The salesman instead told Burnett that the homes were not yet for sale to blacks. Burnett and his wife were crushed that they could not be a part of the community because of the color of their skin.

The Anti-Defamation League says that throughout history, wars and governments have been affected by racism. Laws have also been based on racist ideas.

George Frederickson, a researcher, writes that the word *racism* is misused. People often use it when they describe a negative opinion of a group "based on culture, religion, or simply a sense of family."[3] Frederickson believes racism has two parts: differences and power. The sense of difference between two groups may lead one group to seek power over another. Fredrickson notes that a more powerful group might treat the less powerful group badly. They might use "ways that we would regard as cruel or unjust if applied to members of our own group."[4]

Carolus Linnaeus was extremely influential in the science of classifying living things.

Linnaeus and Classifying Humans

Carl Linné was an explorer and scientist in the 1700s. He began classifying living creatures based on how they looked. He wrote his books in the Latin language. He even used a Latin form of his own name, Carolus Linnaeus. He used two-word descriptions for everything he classified. Linnaeus was not the first

Classification

Carolus Linnaeus was born in Råshult, Sweden, on May 23, 1707. As a young man, Linnaeus had a garden and was interested in plants. During the 1730s, he made trips to northern Sweden to gather and describe plants. He then began to create a new system to classify plants. Linnaeus's new system was based on visible physical characteristics. The more two organisms looked alike, the more closely related they were. He also developed the two-part system for naming organisms. It is still used today. He continued his quest to classify organisms until his death in January 1778.

person to try to categorize plants and animals. He is recognized as bringing order to the study of them.

Besides plants and animals, Linnaeus also classified people. He believed they fit into four groups. The groups depended on where they were from and their skin color. He placed humans in the category *Homo sapiens*. Then he subdivided that into other categories. He classified humans into people from the Americas (red skin), Europe (white skin),

Asia (yellow skin), and Africa (dark skin). He believed each group had certain characteristics. For example, he called Asians "melancholy [sad], stiff, and greedy." Europeans were "gentle, optimistic, and inventive."[5] Some people used his divisions of humans as the basis for discussions of race.

Scientists who studied race found Linnaeus's categories confusing. There are as many differences within groups as there are between groups. For example, there are many dark-skinned, dark-haired white people. There are many light-skinned Africans. There are many similarities between Asian peoples and American Indians. This shows that it is not always possible to group people into clear categories.

Race and Ethnicity

Many people confuse race and ethnicity. What some people think of as separate races really are ethnic groups. One definition explains that "most ethnic groups are minority groups with at least some values or institutions that differ from those of the larger society."[6] People within ethnic groups often share a common religion, language, or culture. It makes them feel like part of that group.

Some ethnic groups have been considered to be their own race. The Nazis in Germany considered Jewish people to be a separate race. The Nazis used

Thousands of Jewish people were sent to the Nazi concentration camps because they were Jewish.

this belief to justify their treatment of Jews during World War II. In reality, Jews are not a race. Rather, they are part of an ethnic group. They belong to an even larger group called Semitic peoples. This group also includes people of Arabian descent. The languages of Hebrew, which many Jews speak, and Arabic are Semitic languages.

Recent studies of DNA show there really is no such thing as race in genetics. There is no gene in any group that is not in another group. Instead, people

Die Katze lässt das Mausen nicht?

have used things they can see to judge a person's race. These include skin color, hair color or texture, or eye shape. Many people have believed these "racial" markers are permanent and unchanging. Legal scholar and microbiologist Pilar Ossoria tells us they are not permanent. In fact, they do not even exist. "We can't find any genetic markers that are in everybody of a particular race and in nobody of some other race."[7] In other words, race is not an objective, scientific fact.

Instead, race seems to be an idea that varies at different times and places. For example, anthropologist Alan Goodman writes, "What is black in the United States is not what's black in Brazil or what's black in South Africa."[8] In the United States at one time, some groups were not considered white. Today, these same groups—Italians, Jews, or Irish—are considered white.

Legal Definitions

James Horton, a historian, offers evidence that race is only a legal idea:

"[Around 1900] Virginia law defined a Black person as a person with one-sixteenth African ancestry. Now Florida defined a Black person as a person with one-eighth African ancestry. Alabama said, 'You're Black if you got any Black ancestry, any African ancestry at all.' But you know what this means? You can walk across a state line and literally, legally change race."[9]

Chapter 2

PREJUDICE AND STEREOTYPES

Linnaeus sorted people according to their physical characteristics. This sorting became the basis for what people thought of as races. Linnaeus and his descriptions led Europeans to see their race as superior to other races.

Later scientists also investigated the question of race. Most scientists studying race at that time were from Europe. Non-Europeans were often considered "primitive." They were seen as inferior to Europeans and their cultures.

This attitude led to racist behavior. Racist behavior is based on differences and power. Europeans used the idea as a reason to seize power over others. For them, one's whiteness became the standard of how successful one could be. Many whites believed they were helping improve the "lesser" races by ruling over them. Later generations sometimes

Some Americans hold tightly to extremist views and generalize about race and ethnicity.

called this belief the "white man's burden."

These ideas of race have led to discrimination and prejudice. The Merriam-Webster dictionary defines discrimination as "prejudiced or prejudicial outlook, action, or treatment."[1] According to writer Brian Cronk, prejudice is "an opinion formed without taking the time or care to judge fairly."[2] Prejudice and discrimination are forms of intolerance. Although racism often causes intolerance, it is not the only cause.

"White Man's Burden"

British poet Rudyard Kipling was a believer in the "white man's burden." He even wrote a poem about it. He described how the white man knew what was best for other people. The white man would help those people even if they blamed and hated the whites. He used phrases such as "half devil and half child" that showed others as evil or unable to help themselves.[3]

Stereotyping

A major cause of prejudice and intolerance is stereotyping. This happens when someone judges an entire group of people. They do this using simplified, sometimes inaccurate, ideas. A person believes that all members of a stereotyped group have certain behaviors or ideas.

Stereotypes usually occur because of fear, ignorance, or laziness. When someone is afraid of another group, the person may stereotype that group's members. The person may see that another group behaves in unfamiliar ways. Instead of finding out why the group behaves that way, the person might rely on stereotypes. It can be easier and more comfortable

This young civil rights demonstrator was attacked by police dogs during a 1963 protest in Birmingham, Alabama.

to use stereotypes than to find out true information about others.

We learn stereotypes as children. We often carry them deep inside us. Movies, television shows, or other media outlets give us images of people. These may influence how we view groups. For example, some early television shows depicted minority members in roles of laborers or domestic servants. This might influence the way people think about minority members.

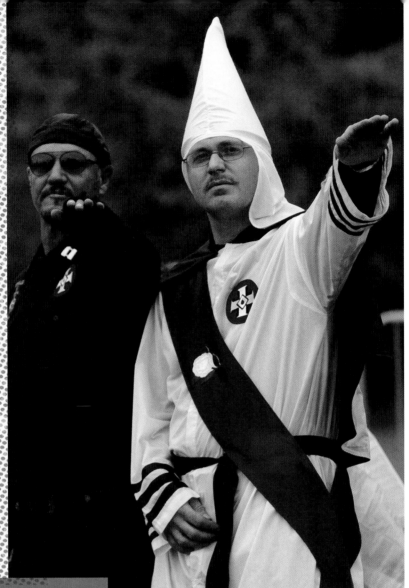

The Ku Klux Klan organization has spread widely outside the United States.

A more important source of information about stereotypes is the family. We often learn stereotypes while we are quite young. As a result, we may grow up "knowing" that the stereotypes are true.

Passed Down

Racism is learned by children from the adults around them. A song from a 1949 musical play, *South Pacific*, describes that process:
You've got to be taught before it's too late,
Before you are six or seven or eight,
To hate all the people your relatives hate,
You've got to be carefully taught![4]

Children with these thoughts grow into adults who keep the stereotypes going. They do not question the beliefs. It is often difficult to recognize our stereotypes about others. It is especially hard when we join together only with people who have similar ideas. At some point, most people make a first trip away from home. The trip may be to attend a college in a different region or to travel in a foreign country. This may help people to learn that not everyone looks at other people in the same way.

But there are ways to combat stereotypes, especially racial ones. The Conflict Information Consortium at the University of Colorado was founded in 1988. The organization wanted to research ways that conflict could be resolved. They suggest that to combat stereotypes, people can take extra steps

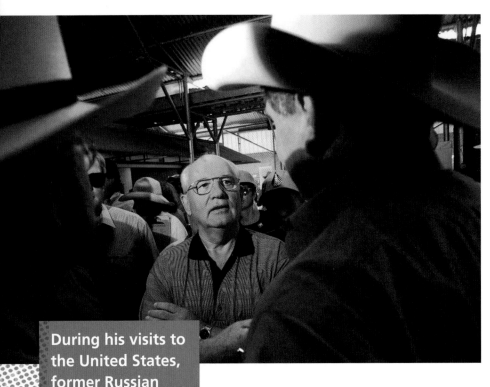

During his visits to the United States, former Russian president Mikhail Gorbachev was warm and friendly.

to act in a manner opposite of their stereotype. For example, when Russian leader Mikhail Gorbachev first visited the United States, many people thought he would be cold and harsh. However, he was warm and accepting. His actions proved his stereotype wrong.

Using stereotypes makes people seem less human. This might make it easier to disrespect them. It might also make it easier to treat them badly. Racism and prejudice produce ill treatment of others. They exist worldwide—including in the United States.

Chapter 3

U.S. RACISM AND AFRICAN AMERICANS

The United States is proud of its justice and equality. It has stood for human rights. It has helped other countries during wars and disasters. It has protected the innocent. Its founding document, the Declaration of Independence, proclaims "all men are created equal."[1]

However, U.S. history also has given examples of unjust and unfair situations. Racism and prejudice stepped ashore in North America with the first Europeans.

The First U.S. Slaves

The English began to settle in North America in the early 1600s. The first permanent English settlement was Jamestown. It lay in what is now the state of Virginia. In 1619, a Dutch ship arrived at Jamestown. It carried Africans. The Dutch sold them as

Africans were captured into slavery and sold in the United States until the 1800s.

indentured servants. Indentured servants usually worked for a master for seven years. They received no pay. But the master taught them a trade, such as carpentry. At the end of seven years, the servants had fulfilled the contract. The servants were then free.

At that time, color did not seem to be the deciding factor of status. Rather, wealth and class separated people into social groups. Most of the poorest people in the English colonies were white indentured servants.

By the late 1600s, though, African slavery was fully accepted in the English colonies in America. Slaveholders saw Africans as a separate race from white Europeans. Some white slaveholders believed that Africans and their enslaved descendants were like helpless children. If these slaves did not belong to white slaveholders, who would take care of them?

By the time of Thomas Jefferson and the American Revolution (1775–1783), "slavery had become so widespread that to many whites it seemed the natural state for black people."[2]

The Bible and Slavery

The words of the Christian Apostle Paul have caused conflict over slavery. In Ephesians 6:5, Paul wrote, "Slaves, obey your earthly masters ...as you would obey Christ." Many believe this shows slavery is acceptable. Yet, Paul says a few lines later, "And masters, . . . do not threaten them." In another letter, Paul places slave traders among the worst sinners, including murderers, liars, and godless people (1 Timothy 1:8–10).[3]

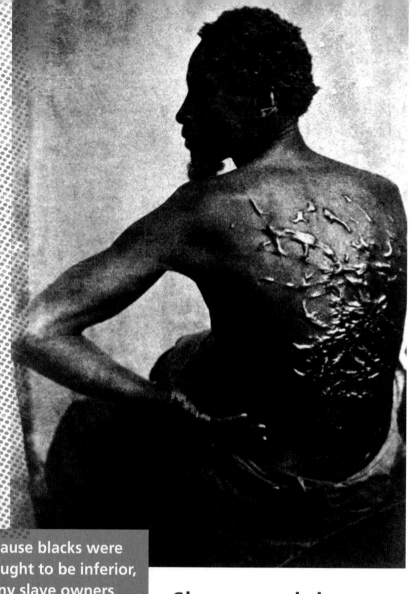

Because blacks were thought to be inferior, many slave owners whipped and beat their black slaves.

Slavery and the Declaration of Independence

The issue of slavery continued to cause conflict in the United States. Even the writers of the Declaration of Independence had mixed feelings about it. Thomas Jefferson wanted to include the idea that slavery was "a cruel war against human nature itself."[4] Yet Jefferson kept slaves himself. Congressional representatives who held slaves objected to the language. The phrase was removed from the July 4, 1776, Declaration of Independence.

Some leaders of the American Revolution still hoped slavery would be outlawed. George Washington wanted Virginia to end slavery. Washington's influence, however, did not help end slavery in his lifetime.

Colin Powell on the Declaration of Independence

Colin Powell is the former head of the Joint Chiefs of Staff. He is an African American. He once commented about the Declaration of Independence. He called it "one of the most remarkable documents in the world." About the phrase *inalienable rights*, he said they are rights "given to you by God, so they can't be taken away."[5]

This black man was lynched in 1935 for allegedly attacking a white woman.

The Civil War and Reconstruction

The issue of slavery was not settled until the U.S. Civil War (1861–1865). By about 1860, nearly 4 million people were enslaved in the United States. The war began over the right of states to be free of interference from the federal government. The Northern states won the war. The United States remained united. Slavery was ended.

After the war's end, lawmakers wanted to make sure the former slaves remained free. So they

The Emancipation Proclamation

President Abraham Lincoln wanted to end slavery. But at the start of the Civil War, he had to be careful.

Four slave states joined the Union. They were Delaware, Kentucky, Maryland, and Missouri. If Lincoln declared all slaves free, the four states might have left the Union. They might have fought for the South. Instead, Lincoln issued the Emancipation Proclamation. It was issued in September 1862, after a year of war. It said that all slaves in areas under Southern control were free as of January 1, 1863. That meant the four slave states in the North could keep their slaves. The proclamation did not free any slaves right away. However, it convinced France and Britain not to help the South. Those countries had already ended slavery.

passed several amendments to the U.S. Constitution. The Constitution is the highest law of the land. The Congress passed the Thirteenth Amendment in 1865.

The amendment was then ratified by the states. This change to the Constitution permanently outlawed slavery in the United States and anywhere under U.S. control. It stated, "Neither slavery nor involuntary servitude . . . shall exist within the United States, or any place subject to their jurisdiction."[6]

Segregation demonstrated a fear and reluctance to combine people of different colors in public places.

Many Southern whites did not want their children to attend schools with blacks.

The years from 1865 to 1877 were known as the Reconstruction era. The United States was to be rebuilt after the war's destruction. There was a lot of rebuilding to be done in the South. Congress passed many laws to help former enslaved African Americans. But some Southerners still considered African Americans less human than whites. Whites were determined to hold onto power. Many thought giving former slaves rights might lessen white power. Southern whites held many racist views, including the belief that "whites were born superior to blacks with respect to intelligence, talents, and moral standards."[7]

From about 1870 to the mid-1950s, separation between whites and African Americans was deeply embedded. Whites continued to hold power. African Americans were kept in poverty. In many states, the law said the two groups had to be kept apart. This was called segregation. According to historian Alton Hornsby Jr., the U.S. Supreme Court determined segregation was acceptable. In 1896, in the case of *Plessy v. Ferguson*, the court argued that "segregation in itself did not represent inequality and that separate public facilities could be provided for the races as long as the facilities were equal." This case showed

Separate but Equal

Jim Crow laws were passed to keep whites and African Americans legally separated. The name came from an African-American character in a song from the 1830s. For example, laws did not allow African Americans to use the same water fountains as whites. African Americans could not eat at restaurants reserved for whites. By the 1950s and 1960s, the U.S. Supreme Court said Jim Crow laws were no longer legal.

Many blacks boycotted restaurants and other segregated places. Some even picketed against the Jim Crow laws.

an acceptance of separation between the races. But the truth was, "nearly all the separate schools, places of recreation, and other public facilities provided for blacks were far inferior to those provided for whites."[8] "Separate but equal" continued until 1954.

Chapter 4

U.S. RACISM AND INTOLERANCE TOWARD OTHER GROUPS

Racism and intolerance are directed not only at African Americans. Other groups in the United States have also been targets of racist hate.

In 1848, James Wilson Marshall discovered gold in California. The discovery drew tens of thousands of gold seekers to California. It brought white Americans from the eastern United States. It also brought thousands of Chinese who hoped to find gold and become rich.

Henry Norton, writing in 1924, noted that the first Chinese to arrive at the gold fields were welcomed. This lasted, Norton says, "as long as the surface gold was plentiful enough to make rich all who came. But that happy situation was not long to continue."[1]

When gold became harder to find, whites turned against the Chinese. Chinese were easily recognizable and did not know the legal system. It was easy to attack them legally and physically. It was easy to pass laws against them. For example, the Foreign Miners' License Law of 1850 charged non-U.S. citizens $20 a month to mine gold. That was too expensive for many Chinese. They were forced out of the gold fields.

In 1852, California Governor John Bigler declared that Chinese were a menace to the state. That caused an increase in anti-Chinese activity. This official support of racist intolerance increased physical violence against Chinese. It also increased legal actions.

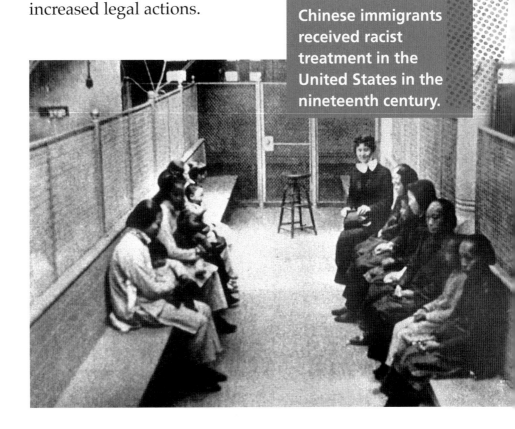

Chinese immigrants received racist treatment in the United States in the nineteenth century.

This drawing represents the violence against Chinese laborers in Rock Springs, Wyoming, in 1885.

In 1854, some Chinese wanted to testify in a murder case in California. The man they wanted to speak against was white. The Chinese were not allowed to testify. The judge was concerned. He said, "The same rule which would admit them to testify, would admit them to all the equal rights of citizenship, and we might soon see them at the polls, in the jury box, upon the bench, and in our legislative halls."[2] The judge clearly stated that Chinese were not the equals of whites.

The same attitude placed very low limits on the number of Chinese who could enter the United States. In 1882, the U.S. government passed the Chinese Exclusion Act. This law kept nearly all Chinese out of the United States for ten years. The law was renewed after that as the Geary Act. Chinese who lived in the United States before the act could not become U.S. citizens until 1943. All Chinese inside the United States had to carry identity passes.

Chinese Exclusion Act, May 6, 1882

"Be it enacted by the Senate and House of Representatives of the United States of America in Congress assembled, That from and after the expiration of ninety days next after the passage of this act, and until the expiration of ten years next after the passage of this act, the coming of Chinese laborers to the United States be, and the same is hereby, suspended; and during such suspension it shall not be lawful for any Chinese laborer to come, or having so come after the expiration of said ninety days, to remain within the United States."[3]

Intolerance Toward Japanese

Japanese people were brought to California in the 1860s. They were to be used as contract workers. They were not expected to stay in the country permanently. White citizens were suspicious of them. They tried to exclude them with laws similar to those applied to the Chinese. The California government passed a law in 1913 that Japanese could not buy property outside certain areas. Not only in California, but also nationwide, Japanese were being discriminated against. The court case of *Takao Ozawa v. United States* allowed states to deny Japanese the right to become U.S. citizens.

Not a Traitor

Takao Ozawa argued that he was as American as anyone else. He also stated that he was a better American than some who had been born in the country: "In name, General Benedict Arnold was an American, but at heart he was a traitor. In name, I am not all American, but at heart I am an American."[4] The court was not convinced.

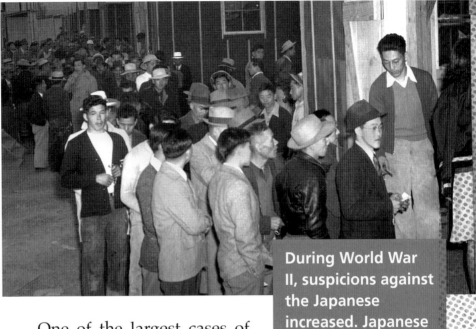

During World War II, suspicions against the Japanese increased. Japanese on the West Coast were forced into internment camps.

One of the largest cases of discrimination against Japanese in the United States occurred during World War II. In 1941, Japanese airplanes attacked the U.S. naval base in Pearl Harbor, Hawaii. Suspicion and distrust of the Japanese reached a high level. President Franklin Roosevelt signed Executive Order 9066. This created "internment camps." These camps were really prisons. They were used to imprison all Japanese Americans along the West Coast. They were imprisoned because of fears that they would spy for the Japanese. The governor of Wyoming expressed the view of many white Americans. He said, "If you bring Japanese into my state, I promise you they will be

hanging from every tree."[5] Between 110,000 and 120,000 men, women, and children were placed in ten detention camps. Many of these people lost their homes and property. Thousands of Japanese Americans fought for the U.S. military. And despite that, Japanese living in the United States were not allowed to become U.S. citizens until 1952.

Intolerance Toward American Indians

Thomas Jefferson admired the American Indians. He said they were equal to whites in intelligence.

George Fredrickson, a historian, says, "The original view of the Indians was that they were naturally white people, and they looked slightly brown because of exposure to the sun and because of the way they treated their skin."[6] But this positive view changed. As the United States expanded its borders, it needed land for settlers. Planters in the South needed land to expand cotton and other crops. The Indians who lived in areas where settlers were entering were legally and physically threatened. Eventually, they were forced to give up their lands.

> The United States seized land from American Indians. Many believed that the Indians were inferior to white-skinned people.

By the 1830s, U.S. opinion was that Indians were savages. U.S. President Andrew Jackson proposed that all Indians east of the Mississippi River be moved west of it. He believed they would become extinct if not moved. He did not think that Indians could live alongside whites. Some Indians resisted removal. The army forced them into Indian Territory, which is present-day Oklahoma.

The Cherokee nation attempted to avoid this removal by adopting white ways. They became farmers, became Christians, and learned English. They created a constitution patterned on the U.S.

Constitution. But the pressure for them to leave their land continued. They resisted the attempts of settlers to take their land. But the U.S. Army forced them off. Approximately 16,000 Cherokee had to walk from Georgia to Indian Territory. The distance was about 1,000 miles (1,600 km). The journey became known as the Trail of Tears. Along the way, hundreds died.

Indian Gaming

The territory of what is present-day Minnesota was once split between the Ojibwa and the Sioux. The two nations signed an agreement with the U.S. government in 1825. It gave all the land to these two peoples. But later in the 1800s, the land was opened to white settlers. The two Indian nations were pushed onto much smaller reservations. Today, the Shakopee Mdewakanton Sioux Community is buying back some of that land. The community allows gambling on its reservation lands and has built two casinos. Gamblers, who are mainly white, spend millions of dollars in the tribal-owned community. The nation has bought about 2,000 acres of neighboring land.

These sculptures are on display in a Cherokee museum in Tahlequah, Oklahoma. The sculptures depict the journey west, where thousands of Cherokee perished as the tribes were forced to relocate.

Thousands more died after they reached their new home.

This set a pattern that continued into the 1900s. Supporters of the westward movement argued that the West was for whites alone. They said that whites were the only ones who deserved the land. Anyone who was not white could be forced off the land. This included Indians and Mexicans. They believed killing or mistreating these groups was not quite the same as killing a "real human."

Chapter 5

DEALING WITH RACISM AND INTOLERANCE

The history of U.S. racism, discrimination, and intolerance is long. But many attempts have been made to improve the situation. The *Plessy v. Ferguson* court case ruled that "separate but equal" facilities were legal. In 1954, the U.S. Supreme Court made a different court ruling. In *Brown v. Board of Education,* the court said segregation in schools was not constitutional. This marked the beginning of the end of racial segregation. It still took many years before most social institutions were integrated. Some people argue that the process still continues today.

The ruling also signaled the start of the civil rights era. During this time, laws were passed to help people overcome America's racist past. Voting laws helped African Americans vote more easily. The Civil Rights Act of 1968 helped minority groups in buying or renting housing.

Generation to Generation

"If you as parents cut corners, your children will too. If you lie, they will too. If you spend all your money on yourselves and tithe no portion of it for charities, colleges, churches, synagogues, and civic causes, your children won't either. And if parents snicker at racial and gender jokes, another generation will pass on the poison adults still have not had the courage to snuff out."[1]

—*Marian Wright Edelman*

One landmark was the Civil Rights Act of 1964. It "bans discrimination because of a person's color, race, national origin, religion, or sex. The act primarily protects the rights of blacks and other minorities."[2] President Lyndon Johnson supported the proposed law. But before it could be enacted as a law, Congress had to vote on it. A 75-day filibuster occurred before it passed. A filibuster is a long debate meant to block a vote on a law. This was one of the longest filibusters in the history of the U.S. Senate.

In 1965, President Lyndon Johnson gave a speech at Howard University. The university is in Washington DC. President Johnson described why he agreed with laws such as the Civil Rights Act of 1964. He said, "Freedom is not enough. You do not wipe away the scars of centuries by saying: Now you are free to go where you want, and do as you desire, and choose the leaders you please. . . . Thus it is not enough just to open the gates of opportunity. All our citizens must have the ability to walk through those gates."[3]

The Civil Rights Act of 1964 also established the Equal

President Lyndon Johnson signed the Civil Rights Act in 1964.

Employment Opportunity Commission (EEOC). If an individual feels he or she has been discriminated against, they can contact the EEOC. This includes discrimination based on race, age, religion, gender, or other reasons.

During the 1970s, the government began affirmative action. Affirmative action is a system that helps minorities have the same opportunities as everyone else. Some measures include hiring women and members of minority groups. Minority workers also receive special training. Businesses that worked with the government needed to set up such plans. For example, a company that manufactured airplane parts for the U.S. Air Force was required to hire a certain number of minority members.

Some people, however, are against the affirmative action programs. They argue that it is unfair in a hiring situation, for example. They say that the employer should hire the most qualified person for the job, no matter what race or gender that person is. Some people even call it reverse discrimination. They say that it might cause discrimination against non-minority members.

Racism and Intolerance Worldwide

Many countries around the world have recognized the unfairness of racism. These countries know that racism can lead to injury, harm, and even death. Some countries have experienced the destruction racism can cause. For example, South Africa's formerly racist government led to many years of separation and injustice. Individual governments have set up constitutions to protect people from racism and other crimes.

Racism has also led to many instances of genocide. The United Nations (UN) considers genocide to be any act that intends to destroy a

Apartheid is the term used to describe the segregation in South Africa.

national, ethnic, racial, or religious group. Genocide has occurred at many times in history. One example is the mass killing of the Jews under Nazi Germany.

The UN has passed international conventions against racism. A convention is a set of rules that countries agree to follow. The best-known convention comes from the UN High Commissioner for Human Rights. It was passed in 1948. The Convention on the Prevention and Punishment of the Crime of Genocide defines genocide. It also describes what types of punishment can be given. Some people

Convention Concerns

The United States and most other countries have signed the Convention on the Prevention and Punishment of the Crime of Genocide. However, the U.S. government worries that the convention could outweigh U.S. considerations for individual rights such as freedom of speech. The government said it would accept the convention as far as it does not restrict any rights that are defended by the United States Constitution or other laws. Many other countries have expressed similar doubts about the convention.

If it is not dealt with, racist acts and attitudes can lead to genocide, such as the Holocaust.

claim the convention is useless. They point out it was first enforced in the 1990s—50 years after it was adopted. The convention was used to convict leaders of Rwanda, in Africa. Genocide had occurred when members of the Hutu tribe slaughtered members of the Tutsi tribe.

One prominent institution that has been set up is the International Court of Justice in The Hague. The Hague is located in the Netherlands. It is also called the World Court. The court is part of the UN. It is the latest in a series of attempts to have an international court.

The Rwandan genocide is another example of what stereotypes and generalizations can lead to.

The attempts began in the late 1800s. Not every country accepts its decisions. As writer Robert J. Pranger points out, "nations do not submit cases to the court unless they are prepared to accept its decisions."[4]

One famous case involved the former leader of Serbia, Slobodan Milosevic. He was charged with crimes against humanity. These crimes were committed during the civil war that took place after the breakup of the former Yugoslavia. Milosevic was arrested in 2001. He was then brought to trial before the World Court. He died in 2006 of a heart attack before the trial ended. His death "dashed hopes that he would be held accountable for the death of more than 200,000 people."[5]

Do Not Be Discouraged

Racism and intolerance have long been a problem. These issues have been experienced in the United States and throughout the world. Discrimination has occurred for centuries.

However, many groups have made progress in their fights for equality. Recognizing that racism is not a scientific fact but rather a social idea can make the fight easier. But there is still much work to be done. On August 28, 1963, civil rights leader Martin Luther King Jr. said, "I have a dream that one day this nation will rise up and live out the true meaning of its creed: 'We hold these truths to be self-evident: that all men are created equal.'"[6] Laws have helped begin to realize that dream.

African-American writer James Baldwin was unhappy with racial relations in America. He spoke for many people in warning that "if we . . . do not falter in our duty now, we may be able . . . to end the racial nightmare."[7]

Today, racism is still a problem. Hatewatch tracks hate groups in the United States. Hate groups include

Martin Luther King Jr. was an advocate for civil rights. His vision for racial equality gives us something to strive for even today.

the Ku Klux Klan, neo-Nazis, and racist skinhead groups. Many of these groups commit hate crimes. Hate crimes are crimes that are aimed at a particular race, gender, or group. Hatewatch also advocates for racial equality in the government, the military, and other places. There are numerous organizations in the United States that continue to work for civil and human rights.

You may find evidence of racist behavior at your school or community. Have you ever heard someone insult a member of another group? Have you ever seen racist graffiti? If we take steps to consider others and look at the bigger picture, we can influence those around us and do our part to lessen racist mindsets. Each person can make a difference.

Glossary

Convention
A set of rules that countries agree to follow.

Discrimination
Prejudiced views, actions, or treatment of others.

Emancipation Proclamation
A statement by Abraham Lincoln that all slaves in Confederate-controlled areas were free. The Emancipation Proclamation led the way to ending U.S. slavery.

Ethnic Group
People who often share a common religion, language, or culture.

Genocide
Any act meant to destroy a national, ethnic, or religious group; sometimes called "ethnic cleansing."

Inalienable Rights
Rights that cannot be taken away.

Indentured Servant
Someone who works for a master in exchange for learning a trade or living costs.

Intolerance

Treating others with hate or with unwillingness to grant them rights.

Jim Crow Laws

Laws that kept whites and African Americans apart.

News Media

Sources of news, including television, radio, the Internet, and newspapers.

Prejudice

An opinion formed without just grounds or knowledge.

Racism

Poor treatment of others based on the belief that they are inferior.

Segregation

The act of separating people of different races.

Stereotype

Judging an entire group of people using simplified, often inaccurate, ideas.

More Information

Books

Carnes, Jim. *Us and Them: A History of Intolerance in America.* New York: Oxford University Press, 1999.

Cooper, Adrian. *Racism.* Chicago: Raintree, 2003.

George, Charles. *Life Under the Jim Crow Laws.* Farmington Hills, MI: Greenhaven Press, 2000.

Marsico, Katie. *Racism.* Ann Arbor, MI: Cherry Lake, 2008.

Sanders, Pete. *Dealing With Racism.* North Mankato, MN: Stargazer, 2007.

Web Sites

Anti-Defamation League (www.adl.org). The Anti-Defamation League was founded to stop anti-Semitism. The organization now exists to protect human rights for all.

California Newsreel—Race: The Power of an Illusion (www.newsreel.org/transcripts/race1.htm). This site contains the transcript of a documentary film that set out to discuss and study the idea of race.

Southern Poverty Law Center (www.splcenter.org). The Southern Poverty Law Center is located in Montgomery, Alabama, and began as a civil rights law firm. The SPLC now teaches tolerance and fights against hate groups.

Notes

Chapter 1. What Is Racism?

1. "Racism." *Merriam-Webster Online Dictionary*. 6 May 2008 <http://www.merriam-webster.com/dictionary/racism>.

2. "Mission Statement." *Anti-Defamation League*. 17 May 2008 <http://www.adl.org/about.asp>.

3. George M. Frederickson. *Racism: A Short History*. Princeton, NJ: Princeton University Press, 2003. 5.

4. Ibid. 9.

5. "Race." *MSN Encarta Online Encyclopedia*. 9 May 2008 <http://encarta.msn.com/encyclopedia_761576599_2/race.html>.

6. Thomas F. Pettigrew. "Ethnic group." *World Book Online Reference Center*. 20 May 2008 <http://www.worldbookonline.com/wb/Article?id=ar185770>.

7. *Race: The Power of an Illusion*. Episode One: "The Difference Between Us." *California Newsreel*. 15 May 2008 <http://www.newsreel.org/transcripts/race1.htm>.

8. Ibid.

9. *Race: The Power of an Illusion*. Episode Three: "The House We Live In." *California Newsreel*. 15 May 2008 <http://www.newsreel.org/transcripts/race3.htm>.

Chapter 2. Prejudice and Stereotypes

1. "Discrimination." *Merriam-Webster Online Dictionary*. 9 May 2008 <http://www.merriam-webster.com/dictionary/discrimination>.

2. Brian Cronk. "Prejudice." *World Book Online Reference Center* 11 May 2008 <http://www.worldbookonline.com/wb/Article?id=ar444320>.

3. Rudyard Kipling. "The White Man's Burden." *The Literature Network*. 9 May 2008 <http://www.online-literature.com/kipling/922/>.

4. Oscar Hammerstein II. "Carefully Taught." *South Pacific*. New York: Williamson Music, 1949.

Chapter 3. U.S. Racism and African Americans

1. "The Declaration of Independence." *ushistory.org*. 10 July 2008 <http://www.ushistory.org/declaration/document/index.htm>.
2. *Race: The Power of an Illusion*. Episode One: "The Difference Between Us." *California Newsreel*. 15 May 2008 <http://www.newsreel.org/transcripts/race1.htm>.
3. "Ephesians 6." *Blueletterbible.com*. New International Version. 25 June 2008 <http://www.blueletterbible.org/cgi-bin/tools/printer-friendly.pl?translation=niv&book=Eph&chapter=6#top>.
4. Thomas Jefferson. "Rough draft of the Declaration of Independence." *Africans in America*. PBS. 13 May 2008 <http://www.pbs.org/wgbh/aia/part2/2h33.html>.
5. Colin Powell. "Colin Powell on the Declaration of Independence and how it applied to black people." *Africans in America*. PBS. 13 May 2008 <http://www.pbs.org/wgbh/aia/part2/2i1601.html>.
6. "Constitution of the United States Amendments XI–XXVII." *Avalon Law Project at Yale University*. 13 May 2008 <http://www.yale.edu/lawweb/avalon/amend1.htm#13>.
7. "First Years of Freedom." *World Book Online Reference Center*. 13 May 2008 <http://www.worldbookonline.com/wb/Article?id=ar006745>.
8. Ibid.

Chapter 4. U.S. Racism and Intolerance Toward Other Groups

1. Henry K. Norton. "The Story of California from the Earliest Days to the Present." Chicago: A. C. McClurg, 1924. 283–296. *Virtual Museum of the City of San Francisco*. 14 May 2008 <http://www.sfmuseum.org/hist6/chinhate.html>.
2. California State Supreme Court. *The People, Respondent, v. George W. Hall, Appellant*, 1854. 14 May 2008 <http://academic.udayton.edu/race/03justice/case0001.htm>.
3. "Chinese Exclusion Act." *Avalon Project at Yale Law School*. 14 May 2008 <http://www.yale.edu/lawweb/avalon/statutes/chinese_exclusion_act.htm>.

4. Frank H. Wu. "Where Are You Really From?: Asian Americans and the Perpetual Foreigner Syndrome." *Civil Rights Journal.* Winter 2002. 20 May 2008 <http://findarticles.com/p/articles/mi_m0HSP/is_1_6/ai_106647778/pg_6>.

5. Nels Smith. "The War Relocation Authority and the Incarceration of Japanese-Americans During WWII." *Harry S. Truman Library and Museum.* 13 May 2008 <http://www.trumanlibrary.org/whistlestop/study_collections/japanese_internment/1942.htm>.

6. *Race: The Power of an Illusion.* Episode Two: "The Story We Tell." *California Newsreel.* 15 May 2008 <http://www.newsreel.org/transcripts/race2.htm>.

Chapter 5. Dealing with Racism and Intolerance

1. Karen Weekes, compiler. *Women Know Everything!: 3,241 Quips, Quotes, and Brilliant Remarks.* Philadelphia: Quirk Books, 2007. 346.

2. Charles V. Hamilton. "Civil Rights Act of 1964." *World Book Online Reference Center.* 17 May 2008 <http://www.worldbookonline.com/wb/Article?id=ar116995>.

3. Lyndon B. Johnson. "President Lyndon B. Johnson's Commencement Address at Howard University 'To Fulfill These Rights,' June 4, 1965." *Lyndon Baines Johnson Library and Museum.* 7 May 2008 <http://www.lbjlib.utexas.edu/johnson/archives.hom/speeches.hom/650604.asp>.

4. Robert J. Pranger. "International Court of Justice." *World Book Online Reference Center.* 8 May 2008 <http://www.worldbookonline.com/wb/Article?id=ar279080>.

5. "Slobodan Milosevic." *Information Please.* 17 May 2008 <http://www.infoplease.com/ipa/A0771127.html>.

6. Martin Luther King, Jr. "Papers Project." *Martin Luther King, Jr., Research and Education Institute.* Stanford University. 17 May 2008 <http://www.stanford.edu/group/King/>.

7. James Baldwin. *The Fire Next Time.* New York: Vintage Books, 1993. 105–106.

Index

affirmative action, 48
American Indians, 12, 40–44
American Revolution, 25, 27
Anti-Defamation League, 9
Apostle Paul, 25

Baldwin, James, 53
Bigler, John, 35
Brown v. Board of Education, 45
Burnett, Eugene, 7–8

Chinese, 34–37, 38
Chinese Exclusion Act (Geary
  Act), 37
civil rights, 7, 45, 53
Civil Rights Act, 45, 46–48
classification, 10–12
Cronk, Brian, 17

Declaration of Independence,
  23, 26–27
discrimination, 4, 17, 38, 45,
  46, 48, 53

Emancipation Proclamation,
  29
Equal Employment
  Opportunity Commission,
  48
ethnicity, 12–13, 50
Executive Order 9066, 39

Foreign Miners' License Law,
  35
Frederickson, George, 9

genocide, 49–51
Goodman, Alan, 15
Gorbachev, Mikhail, 22

Hatewatch, 53–55
Hornsby, Alton, Jr., 32
Horton, James, 15

indentured servants, 24
Indian Territory, 42, 43
International Court of Justice,
  51
"internment camps," 39

Jackson, Andrew, 42. *See also*
  American Indians
Jamestown, 23
Japanese, 38–40. *See also*
  "internment camps"
Jefferson, Thomas, 25, 27, 40
Jews, 4, 9, 12–13, 15, 50
Jim Crow laws, 32
Johnson, Lyndon, 46–47

King, Martin Luther, Jr., 53
Kipling, Rudyard, 18
Ku Klux Klan, 54

Lincoln, Abraham, 29
Linné, Carl (Carolus
  Linnaeus), 10–12

Marshall, James Wilson, 34
Milosovec, Slobodan, 52

Nazis, 4, 12–13, 50, 54
news media, 7, 19
Norton, Henry, 34

Ossoria, Pilar, 14
Ozawa, Takao, 38

Pearl Harbor, 39
Plessy v. Ferguson, 32, 45. *See
  also* "separate but equal"
Powell, Colin, 27
Pranger, Robert J., 52
prejudice, 17, 18, 22, 23

race, 5, 7, 12–15, 16–17, 25,
  32–33, 46, 48, 54
Reconstruction, 31
Roosevelt, Franklin, 39

segregation, 32–33, 45
"separate but equal," 32, 33,
  45
slavery, 25, 26–27, 28–30
South Pacific, 21
stereotypes, 18–22

Takao Ozawa v. United States,
  38
Thirteenth Amendment, 29
Till, Emmett, 4–5

U.S. Civil War, 28, 29
United Nations, 49, 50, 51

Washington, George, 27
"white man's burden," 17, 18.
  See also Kipling, Rudyard
World Court, 51, 53
World War II, 4, 8, 13, 39

About the Author

Charles Pederson is a consulting writer, translator, and editor. He has written for and contributed to many fiction and nonfiction publications for both children and adults. A graduate in linguistics, international relations, and German, he has traveled widely. He brings to his work an appreciation of different peoples and cultures. He and his wife, children, dog, and cat live near Minneapolis, Minnesota.

Photo Credits